HIS
EVERYDAY
PROMISES

True stories of God's promise that He
will never leave or forsake us as we
journey through this life.

By NANCY SHOAP

PRESS

May these stories be a
blessing to you. If you
know Jesus may they
encourage you... if not,
may they lead you to
Him.

In His Love,
Nancy Shoop
www.hispromises.com

"I do set my rainbow in the cloud, and it shall be for a token of a covenant between me and the earth."(NIV)
Genesis 9:13

Contents

Foreward

The Christian's walk of faith is, at times, both exhilarating and taxing. Sister Nancy Shoap, for whom I am privileged to serve as Pastor, shares her first hand journey through the trails of life and shows how, as the poem "Footprints in the Sand" illustrates, God is carrying us in our most desperate of times. She takes the scriptures and superimposes them over life's circumstances allowing us to catch a glimpse of how God's children should live in this world.

Nancy calls our attention to God's "omnipresence" as she invites and challenges us to lean, even rely, on Him. These fresh, true to life, stories took place in her life and the lives of those around her and did not go unnoticed. She helps us see God's gentle nudging.

These powerful, yet simple and easy to read, vignettes' would make great sermon illustrations for any minister seeking to help others understand and live in the Word. I see the potential for a devotional guide and Bible-study topics. This work is an extraordinary account of God's work in ordinary people. A must read and guaranteed spiritual pick-me-up!

Brother Earl F. Stovall, Pastor
Ridge Church of the Brethren
Shippensburg, PA 17257

Introduction

In our everyday lives we are faced with countless problems, obstacles, various illnesses and challenges. We do not need to handle these problems alone, because of one of the many promises God has given us in His word that He will never leave us alone. He sent the Comforter to be with us. All we need to do is call upon His name.

When we become overwhelmed, we need to rely on His strength and our faith to help us. We get encouragement by reading His word and asking that He strengthen our faith to overcome any obstacles or hardships we may go through in this life.

"Overcoming Fear" can only happen when we realize God is within us, around us, and over us. Read about an unusual circumstance that gave peace to a seemingly hopeless situation.

"Satan's 3-D's" is a story about how Satan uses his three best tools to put road blocks in our path to try to keep God's word from being shared with others.

The story "With God's Help" is a true story written while I was going through a very difficult time in my life. God used a little black kitten to get my attention and open my eyes, both physically and spiritually.

Since the writing of that story, I attempt each day to include the four pillars of health — which are physical, spiritual, mental, and emotional into my life.

After going through the ordeal, I began to think about past experiences that had occurred in my life and those that friends and family had shared with me. As I reminisced about them, thoughts of how God's love, presence, and protection were so prevalent in each circumstance.

In the story "Outstretched Arms" God showed His mercy by rescuing a little boy from drowning.

"Caught in a Trap" is a story of taking a giant leap of faith, trusting the voice of the master.

God showed His love and protection in the story "Answered Prayer." He saved a family from what could have been a fatal accident. It reminds us that His strength and protection is only a prayer away.

In "Unlikely Angel" you'll read about how three young ladies were protected from a dangerous situation. It is a story reminding us that His angels are attending us each day.

The story "His Presence" is reassurance that the Holy Spirit will guide us as we walk through the valley of death. We will never need to walk alone.

"His Healing" is a story told to me by a very dear friend who is a cancer survivor. The way she handled going through this dreaded disease is an inspiration to others of her faith and trust in God.

"God's Willing Servant" is dedicated to an employee whom I observed while performing her everyday duties. It is how each person we come in contact with should be treated if we are striving to please Jesus.

"Divine Intervention" reminds us that God already knows the plans he has for each one of us. You simply have to wait for His timing to bring it to you!

The last story in this book entitled "Mother's Bible" is dedicated to our Mother. It was written from notes found in her Bible. She persevered in the faith regardless of many difficult situations that she faced in her life. She lived by the words written in Galatians 6:9; "And let us not be weary in well doing: for in due season we shall reap, if we faint not." She always kept a strong faith and trusted Jesus to see her through the difficult times.

She is a great influence in my life, and has taught me to always have a strong faith. She has always been a true example of what Jesus wants each of us to be. When times were difficult she never gave up. She trusted Jesus to see her through the situation.

Special thanks to my husband Dave, who was a great help in the writing of these stories. His input, suggestions and ideas he shared with me were greatly appreciated. With his love, patience, and support by reading and editing them, it was possible for this book to become a reality.

Thanks to our pastor Brother Earl for his encouragement for me to share my testimony and the story "With God's Help" to our congregation. It helped me to become stronger and bolder in my faith and walk with the Lord.

Most importantly, I want to give thanks and praise to a loving and compassionate God who used me as a vessel to accomplish the writing this book. When God births something in you, He will take full responsibility to make it everything He wants it to be if you are willing to let Him.

May each of us be encouraged to never give up and talk daily to our Lord. He will help us, in His way and in His time.

Nancy Shoap

Overcoming Fear

…"My peace I give unto you…
Let not your heart be troubled, neither
let it not be afraid."
John 14: 27

Overcoming Fear

Several years ago I was diagnosed with a rare eye condition that causes blindness. It is called posterior uveitis, a disease that is an inflammation of the choroid. The choroid lines the back of the eyes and has many blood vessels. It helps to nourish part of the retina. I went to several specialists who all told me the same thing. Seventy-five percent of persons with this disease go blind.

Various types of drops were prescribed for my eyes, but each one seemed to cause irritation and make my vision worse. After doing some research on my own, I questioned the doctors about this because I did not feel that putting drops in the front of my eyes would help to heal the inflammation located in the back. They all said I was to continue the medications for precautionary measures. I was very sensitive to light. It hurt my eyes and for years I wore dark sunglasses and a visor to keep light from causing pain to my eyes. I endured many harsh comments about this. This caused me to become very depressed. I started to ask, "Why me Lord?" Each day was a struggle for me.

As the years passed my left eye began to close and lost the look of life. What the doctors said was apparently coming true. I was going blind. It was very hard on my husband to be around the person I had become. I had been a very positive person with an up-beat personality.

Years after the diagnosis I thought it was time to prepare for the inevitable. I started to attend a blind support group. Instead of making me feel better about myself, the meetings depressed me more than I already was. So, I quit going and thought whatever the future brings is what I'll have to deal with.

My husband urged me to try one more specialist to see if perhaps they would suggest any different treatment. Approximately one month prior to my appointment I phoned the number of the doctor I had been given. I got a message that basically said, "Hello, leave a message." I thought this was kind of odd for a doctor's office. But I left my message anyway. The message I left was, "Should I discontinue the several different types of drops I was using at this time?" I wanted to know because they would be examining my eyes and I thought perhaps the results would be more accurate if they did not have the medication in them. Several weeks passed and I did not receive an answer. I decided to call again. I got the same message so I left another one asking the same question. My appointment day was getting closer so I made the decision on my own to discontinue the drops.

When I went to the doctor's I asked why they had not answered my phone calls. I was informed that they had never received any. During the routine questions I was asked about any medications I was currently using. I told them none at this time and explained why. The doctor was angry and said, "If you've not been using them you might as well stop them altogether." I did just that. Little did I know that that was the beginning of several miracles in my life.

Approximately one week later, I received a phone call from a lady who said, "I have two messages on my answering machine asking about discontinuing your eye drops." She said, "I don't understand your question." Explaining that she was not a doctor. Now I knew why my messages never reached the doctor.

Looking back now, I call it divine intervention. It was after that incident happened, thanks to God; I no longer had the irritation from the drops. I still had the disease but I now had a peace about it. I put the outcome into His hands and prayed for strength to deal with whatever the future held. My fear of going blind was conquered when I put my absolute dependence and trust in God that His hand would be there to guide me through.

Since that time God has healed me. My vision has been restored and I no longer have to wear the dark sunglasses and a visor because of sensitivity to the light. My left eye is now completely open and looks normal.

God has given a new focus to my life. I felt His calling to be a willing vessel to tell others about His love by writing stories. I believe the obstacles I faced were definitely for my good and resulted in a closer relationship with my Lord. May we always be attuned to Him as we go through difficult times to put our complete trust that He'll carry us. I seize every opportunity to use my gift of new sight to bring glory to Him.

Satan's 3 – D's

DOUBT
DISCOURAGEMENT
DISAPPOINTMENT

"Be sober, be vigilant;
because your adversary the devil,
walketh about, as a roaring lion,
seeking whom he may devour:"
I Peter 5:8

Satan's 3-D's

The story entitled; "With God's Help" became a reality by having to overcome many obstacles of Satan. I experienced doubts, discouragement, and numerous, disappointments. It was written several years ago and accepted by a company for publication. God's hand was in the process from the very beginning.

Following the ordeal, many people told me that I should write the story, because it was truly a miracle. It would encourage, give hope, and inspiration to others that may be going through a difficult time in their lives. I did not feel I had the ability required to perform the task of writing the story.

Approximately one year after the ordeal was over. I would wake up at night and write down things that came to my mind about what had happened. I kept a journal and continually prayed about it. One day I sat down and put the thoughts and phrases into the story, "With God's Help." I kept the story for several months wondering how to share the experience with others and glorify God. Knowing that it was only with His help and guidance I would be able to accomplish this task.

One afternoon I had an appointment with my chiropractor. While sitting in the waiting room, I began reading a book of short stories about animals that go through hard times. Some get lost, some aren't wanted, and some are misunderstood and abused. After reading several of the stories, I turned to the last page of the book where I found an address for the publisher. During my appointment, I continued to think about the book and how much I wanted to read the other stories in it. I asked the chiropractor if she would consider selling the book to me. She said, "Yes." I took it home and read the rest of it. Then turning again to the last page I saw an address written there. I had a feeling that is unexplainable that

I should send the story, "With God's Help" to that address.

Three days later I received a phone call from a lady informing me that she loved the story and wanted to publish it. I was very excited and thanked God for His goodness and guidance.

The next year and a half I kept in constant contact with the editor, who told me that the publication was behind schedule and the book that contained the story should have been completed six months ago. She said she was experiencing some health issues and was unable to work on it as much as she would have liked to.

Then the first obstacle to overcome came my way. The editor no longer answered my calls or faxes. I lost all contact with the progress of the publication. I began to wonder if it would ever become a reality.

For many months Satan used his best tool on me. I started to *doubt* if the story would ever be published. I discussed this with a very good friend, whom gave me words of encouragement telling me not to despair. It would happen in God's time, if it were His will to do so.

Several months past and still I heard nothing. I was standing in my kitchen thinking about the story when I had an overwhelming urge to look through the book where I had found the address originally. Finding a phone number for the company, I called and got a recording to leave a message.

Several days later the senior editor of the company returned my call. She told me that the person who had accepted the story was working for their company as an independent contractor. The reason my calls had not been returned was because that person had been very ill and required surgery. Rehabilitation after surgery did not go well and they had to give up their job.

The workload had been given to someone else. This included the book that contained the story I had written. During the transition of the workload, my address had been given to the person receiving it incorrectly. For approximately one year and a half the company had been trying to contact me. Three letters had been returned with "address unknown" marked on the envelope.

During that period of time, the book had been published and was currently out-of-stock. I was very *discouraged.* Again, Satan used another of his tools on me. First he used doubt and now discouragement.

I waited another four to five months. Finally, one day when I went out to get the mail I received a nice surprise! There was a complimentary copy of the book with my story in it.

I was excited and called the company and ordered ten copies to give as gifts to friends and family. The book contained several short stories of encouragement, of God's love, of hope and inspiration. I wanted to share them with others.

Guess what! Satan did not succeed with doubt and discouragement. Therefore, he tried another of his tools on me. I waited anxiously each day for the order to arrive. Finally, one day approximately one month since I had ordered the books I received the invoice in the mail. But, to my surprise, the books were not included with the order. Was I ever *disappointed!* I called the company and they agreed to reissue the books. This meant additional time of waiting before I would receive them.

Approximately four months later, the books I had ordered to give as gifts finally arrived. I thought that was the end of my ordeal. But, God had other plans for me. Several months later my husband was sharing the story "With God's Help" with our new pastor. Also, he was sharing about my eye condition that is mentioned in that story.

I walked up and joined in the conversation. Our pastor asked if I would share my testimony and the story with our congregation. I said I would sometime. But, again I needed help and courage from God to do it. I was reluctant and felt I did not have the ability.

After hearing many sermons and attending Bible studies where the topic of discussion was about being a willing vessel, I knew God was speaking to me. I took a giant leap of faith and agreed to give my testimony and read the story to our congregation. My husband agreed that he would take part in the presentation. I was very grateful for his help and support. The congregation was encouraged and my husband and I received a blessing from the Lord. A blessing we would have missed if we had refused to be a willing vessel for Him. If we are willing, God is able.

In this life, we are faced with many trials and difficult situations where we encounter; doubt, discouragement, and disappointment. When these occur we have two choices, either draw closer to the Lord or give in to Satan. We draw closer to the Lord by persistent prayer, reading His Word, and waiting patiently for His answer. This will strengthen our faith to stand against the 3D's of Satan. In I Corinthians 1:9 the Bible says, "God is faithful, by whom ye were called unto the fellowship of his Son Jesus Christ our Lord."

As Joshua told the people of Israel in chapter 24, verse 15, ".... choose you this day whom you will serve: ... But as for me and my house, we will serve the Lord." May each of us make that same decision. When we choose to serve the Lord, we have victory over doubt, discouragement, and disappointment as we journey through this life. Then we will also have victory over death and spend eternity with our risen Savior Jesus Christ. The other choice we have is to become bitter with life, give in to Satan and just give up.

God allows Satan to put these roadblocks on the highway of life to teach us His ways and to draw us closer to Him. Satan is the master of the 3D's – *doubt, discouragement,* and *disappointment.*

We must learn to live life one day at a time, and deal with the trials we face with a positive attitude, and a strong faith. God is always able to energize us, even in the midst of life's storms and trials. When we weather the storms of life, we will become stronger in our faith and closer in our walk with Him. He is the miracle of light in darkness, hope in despair, and joy in sorrow. He'll give us quiet peace when life feels as if it's spinning out of control.

God's help is always there when we need it. We have every reason to have faith that He loves us and will care for us. All things are in His time and in His way. His time and His ways are not the same as ours.

"With God's Help", we can enjoy the gift of each new day.

With God's Help

"Take therefore no thought for the morrow: for the morrow shall take thought for the things of itself."
Matt. 6:34

With God's Help

My story began several years ago when I was diagnosed with a rare eye disease that causes blindness. When I was first told, I tried not to show how much it depressed me. I kept myself busy and tried very hard not to think about it. I went to several specialists who all told me the same thing: Seventy-five percent of the people who have this disease go blind. I was not even given a fifty-fifty chance.

One thing I really enjoyed was working in my flower garden. It was there I found solace and talked to the Lord about my feelings. One afternoon while I was working in the flowerbed I heard a meow. There beside me was a small black kitten with green eyes.

I've always heard strays find people lots of times instead of people finding strays. In my case that was what happened. The last thing I wanted was a kitten to take care of. But when he looked at me so helplessly, I had to go into the house and open a can of tuna. It quickly disappeared and the kitten found himself a spot in our garage for sleeping. My husband agreed that we could keep him until he was old enough to fend for himself. My mother suggested that I should litter train him. This was a very easy task.

We guessed his age to be about three and one-half months. Days became months, and "Ace" (that was what we named him) quickly became part of our family. One day a neighbor said, "I know whom your kitten belongs to." I called the family and they said they knew he had come to our house and we could keep him. We did.

At the time I was working fifteen hours a week at our church, so I was not at home as much as my husband, who is retired. Ace became a bosom buddy to him; everywhere he went the kitten followed. Just like a puppy. He was an indoor-outdoor cat. In the daytime he roamed wherever my husband was and at night he slept in our laundry room adjoining our home. We had a squeak toy, which we would squeak, and he would come running. He was such a special animal and we loved him dearly. He truly had his footprints on our hearts.

I really enjoyed taking care of Ace while watching him grow. Several years passed and the small black kitten became an eighteen-pound very large cat.

One day when I came home from work and I asked my husband where Ace was. He replied, "I haven't seen him for about three hours." This was very unusual, but when we squeaked his toy, he didn't come running.

Every day we walked or rode our bicycles through our neighborhood and the surrounding fields looking for him, squeaking his toy, and asking everyone we came in contact with if they had seen Ace. We put up reward posters in the local stores and advertised on our local TV community channel. We called local shelters and animal hospitals. He was not to be found anywhere.

While I was looking for Ace, I was praying for guidance regarding my personal health problems and those of several of my loved ones. It seemed that as I walked looking for Ace I began to really "look" at God's creations. I noticed the beauty of the trees, the mountains, and yes even the flowering weeds. I quit focusing on the diagnosis that I would go blind and began thanking God that I could see as well as I could. I really started to "see" His beauty of creation. My whole attitude began to change. I put it in God's hands and realized what it meant to live life "one day at a time."

My husband and I continued to look for Ace every day, several times a day. This went on for over a month. There was still no sign of Ace anywhere. It was like a part of our family was gone. I just could not bring closure to the situation. The old feelings of depression and despair were beginning to return. I felt God had sent him to me when I needed him and now I could not understand why he was gone without a trace. I called him my black angel, because he had helped me when I needed to gain focus and insight about my life.

My parents, who were both in ill health, had moved into my brother's home where he and his wife were caring for them. My brother and his wife decided to take a month's vacation to her mother's home in another state. They asked my husband and me if we would take care of my parents and their home while they were away. The next day I asked my boss, who was also my pastor, if I could have the month off. He agreed, he knew I was totally devastated.

The week before I was to return to work, my husband and I were spending the day with my parents, and we stopped by our home, which was in the next town. When I went into the house the phone was blinking. It had several messages on it. My neighbor called and said, "I found Ace." Other messages were, "Please call as soon as possible, it is very important." One was from my niece, saying, "Ace is at the animal hospital, but he is in very bad shape. Come in as soon as you get this message." Our neighbor said she was home alone when she heard a wailing sound coming from her basement. It was Ace. She called a friend who had previously worked as a veterinarian assistant and she took him

to the animal hospital. We went there immediately. We were not prepared for what we
found. The cat who had left our home a total
of forty-five days ago weighing eighteen
pounds was now just five pounds, completely
dehydrated, very low temperature, unknown
neurological damages (not seeing, not being
able to eat or make his bowel movements
properly). Although we had not seen Ace for
forty-five days, when my husband spoke to
him and called his name he held out his paws
and meowed in recognition. The veterinarian
said he was too far-gone, and they felt it was
best to euthanize him. They did not know the
extent of the damage internally and he was
too weak to withstand any tests. Judging by
the condition he was in, the veterinarian said
they did not think he would ever see, hear,
or make normal bowel movements again. We
asked them to give him at least twenty-four
hours. They agreed and started re-hydrating
him and giving doses of antibiotics.

I prayed all night long, asking God to spare
him. The next day he was holding his own. We
continued to keep him at the animal hospital
that week. The following day the veterinarian
said he showed a little improvement.

The reason why he was in such bad shape was because he had been in our next-door neighbor's basement the full forty-five days he was missing. The day after he became missing I noticed a broken pane in our neighbor's basement window. I asked them to check and make sure he had not crawled through the broken window. They checked and said; "No," he was not in their basement. Probably he was either too scared or too injured to come when they called him. The next day they repaired the broken window, not knowing that Ace was in their basement. He did not have anything to eat or drink for the next forty-five days. They did not use their basement much, but the few times they did go down, he was too sick, weak or scared to make himself known.

My month's leave was over and it was time for me to return to work, but I just could not keep my mind on it. It no longer seemed as important to me as before. Thank God for a boss who was also my pastor. When I asked him if it was wrong to pray for an animal, he said "No; God wants us to pray about everything that concerns us." He knew how hard my loved ones' illnesses, my health situation, and now this ordeal I was faced with were for me. I continued to pray for guidance.

After much prayer and thought, I realized that God had other plans for me at this time in my life. They were to take care of my loved ones and Ace, and be available to spend more time with them. I resigned from my job at the church.

Ace spent another week at the animal hospital. He showed some progress each day, but he was still very sick. God's guidance was in this ordeal again, because the person who had taken Ace to the hospital said she felt that Ace would do better in his own environment. She offered to show my husband how to re-hydrate him. The veterinarian showed us how to give him a high-calorie gel food supple-ment and some very nasty-tasting antibiotics. We were able to take him home after spending a week at the hospital. We continued to care for him as we were shown.

It was a very slow process, but slowly each month he showed improvement. It was like caring for a newborn baby. At night if he wet or messed in his bed he would cry and I would get up and change the towel he was lying on. After several months he started to eat his regular food. So I knew it was time to re-introduce him to his litter box. One day I heard him scratching and I went in to watch him. He was able to dig a hole, and do his business, but too weak to cover it up. He would fall over in the box from exhaustion. For weeks I would listen for him to scratch and then I would hold him so he would not tire. Finally he was able to go on his own. His eyesight and hearing returned to normal. He continued to eat and put on weight.

Most evenings Ace cuddles up with my husband on the couch, as close as he can get, breaths a sigh of relief, and goes into a very restful sleep— just as we humans can "cuddle in" to our heavenly Father, and rest in His loving and protective arms.

Ace continues to amuse and amaze us each day. This past August we decided to take a short vacation. It was the first time we had been away for any amount of time since Ace's ordeal. I guess he must have sensed we were planning on leaving for a few days, because he tried to keep us from going. He took one of my husband's socks and buried it in his kitty litter box. He was telling us the only way he knew how that he didn't want us to leave him alone.

Our son checked on him every day. We knew he would be very well cared for and we could enjoy a few days of a much needed vacation. But we sure were missed. Ace was so loving, attentive and obedient when we returned. You could tell he was glad we were back.

I am reminded each day about God's love and mercy, and the lessons learned through Ace's ordeal. Seeing him each day being able to see and hear, weighing over twenty pounds, and being a normal cat reminds me constantly that with God's help and strength we can overcome adversities and live our lives one day at a time.

Outstretched Arms

"Thou art my hiding place;
Thou shalt preserve me from trouble;
Thou shalt compass me about
with songs of deliverance."
Psalm 32:7

Outstretched Arms

It was a beautiful summer day. What you would think of as a picture-perfect day. The sky was clear blue, with lots of fluffy white clouds everywhere. The sun was shining and the birds were singing. It seemed liked they too were thanking God for such a wonderful day.

The experience I'm going to share happened about thirty years ago. But, it seems like it just happened yesterday. Our son, Lee who had just turned three years old was in the house with my mother and me. He was on the floor playing with his matchbox cars and very content. He was an only child and he could entertain himself for hours with them.

I remember watching him and thinking how lucky we were to have such a nice little boy. We had two miscarriages prior to his birth and was fortunate that I was able to carry him full term. When he was born he weighed only four pounds. But, he was perfect in every way health wise. Due to health issues I experienced, the doctor did not recommend having any more children. Therefore, you can understand why he was so special to my husband and me.

My mother and I chatted for awhile and then decided it was time to make lunch. We were busy in the kitchen. Lee was in the adjoining room playing. At least that was what we thought. Without us knowing, he had gone to the door and opened it. When he went out into the breezeway he must have heard his grandfather's and his daddy's voices.

They were working just outside the door. They were draining a cistern that had eight to ten feet of dirty water in it. They had the cover off and had pulled the pump up to repair it. It had quit functioning because it was clogged. They wanted to drain the cistern and re-seal the walls.

They said they looked up when they heard Lee's voice. They saw him running as fast as he could towards the two of them. He was unaware of the danger that was in front of him. My husband was kneeling down on his knees at the time. He was cleaning the pump of dirt that had collected in the line and caused the pump to quit working. When he saw Lee he reached out with outstretched arms to catch him. But, he slipped right through them like a basketball through a hoop. He ran full force into the opening of the cistern. Falling headfirst into the dirty water and disappeared from their sight. My husband, who could not swim gave no thought to his own safety. He reacted to the situation by jumping into the dirty water in an effort to save his son from drowning. He was able to locate Lee and handed him safely to the outstretched arms of his grandfather.

His dad carried him into the house and handed him to me. He was cold, shaking, and very scared. He began to vomit the water that he had swallowed. I held him very close and silently prayed for God's help. Mom put warm water in the tub, gently took him from my arms, and put him into the warm water.

I'm sure she was also praying that God would help us in this situation we were facing. She talked softly to Lee, reassuring him that he was safe.

He was very quiet and subdued. Unlike the happy little boy we had seen just minutes before playing with his matchbox cars. We kept him in the warm water for awhile and then wrapped him in a warm blanket. While I was holding him close, his color began to return.

When I think of that frightful day long ago, I'm reminded of the love that God shows to us each day. We know that His eye is on the sparrow, so we know that he will watch over us.

That little boy of thirty years ago is now a man. Just as he enjoyed his matchbox cars then, he now has a passion for real one's today. He keeps each one immaculate and in a garage. His garage looks like a showroom at an auto dealership.

He and his wife enjoy going to car shows and looking at all models, both classic and new. When he was a little boy, he liked to go shopping with his dad and mom to check out all the various models of matchbox cars, he now does the same thing, only on a much larger scale.

When I see how he takes care of his cars today, just like he did his matchbox ones. I'm reminded of God's grace and mercy on that beautiful summer day, when He saved him from drowning. Allowing him to grow up to be the person he is today.

Lee's earthly father was there to rescue him, just as our Heavenly Father is there to rescue each one of us. We need to repent of our sins and receive Him as our Savior. He waits for us with outstretched arms to become His children.

Caught in a Trap

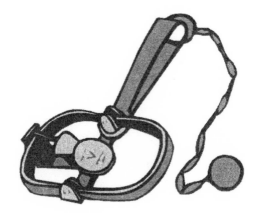

"I can do all things through Christ
which strengtheneth me."
Philippians 4:13

Caught in a Trap

This experience happened to my husband, Dave, his father and two brothers. As he related the story, we talked about how God's hand was in the midst of the situation, with His ever-present help and guidance.

My husband Dave, his father, and two brothers, got up early, packed lunches, and then put their dogs in their cages on the bed of the pickup truck. They left the house with their three dogs, named Barkey, Tony, and Tilly. They were going to let the dogs get some exercise running rabbits and pheasants. Small game season hadn't officially opened yet, so they just wanted to enjoy the day of fun and fellowship with each other and their dogs. As the dogs were trailing rabbits, Dave remarked, "I'm not sure who's enjoying the day more, the dogs running or us watching them have so much fun!"

It was a beautiful cool crisp autumn day. The leaves were showing off their colors of reds, yellows, and oranges. The leaves crackled under foot as they made their way through the fields. God sure had been busy with His paintbrush. His handiwork was very evident in any direction you looked.

They walked the fields for hours, watching the dogs enjoying the day. They saw many rabbits, pheasants, squirrels, chipmunks, and even an occasional ground hog. Dave said, "It felt like God walked with them as they viewed His creation of trees, animals, wildflowers, and yes even the weeds had their own unique beauty."

Before long, the morning was over and they were very hungry. Locating a large shade tree, they unpacked their lunches. After hours of walking, they were ready to replenish themselves with food. Dave said, "It tasted better than a five-star restaurant." It was the atmosphere of being in the great outdoors of

God's creation and the togetherness with his dad and brothers.

They fed and watered the three dogs and put them in their cages for a rest. With the dogs safely in their cages they lay back leisurely on the ground and chatted about the events of the day. The sun on their faces was so warm and relaxing that within minutes they were fast asleep and snoring so loud it could have shaken the mountains in the distance.

They had only been dozing for a short time, but they said it seemed like hours. Dave's brother said, "I actually think we are more tired than the dogs. Now I know what it means to be dog-tired!"

When they awoke, they discussed another place where they could take their dogs to run. They agreed on an area to go to. Driving to their destination, they parked the vehicles, and unloaded the dogs once more. They were ready for more adventure. As the dogs jumped from their cages to the ground, their enthusiasm and excitement was very evident. They were soon on the scent of a rabbit. Their voices could be heard echoing throughout the valley from the

North Mountain to the South Mountain. They were doing their best to please their master. Just as we strive each day to do our very best to please our Master in Heaven.

They ran through a cornfield and picked up the scent of another rabbit. All three dogs were howling and running through the field. Unaware of the dangers they could encounter while enjoying the freedom of running through the open fields.

After a while, only the sound of two of the dogs barking could be heard. Approximately at the same time they looked at each other and said, "Something is wrong with Barkey." He had a very distinct bark and they did not hear it. They became very concerned, especially Dave, sensing the danger that Barkey could possibly be encountering. Barkey was our son's favorite dog. He was the one who had named him Barkey, when we purchased him; he was with a litter of five puppies. He was the only puppy in the group that came up to our son and barked. It was an instant attraction. He said, "Daddy let's take him and call him Barkey." That day Barkey became a part of our family.

When he was not running with the other dogs, our son would play ball with him. He was an only child and Barkey became a great playmate for him. He would spend hours batting the ball and having Barkey run after it and return it to him. You can understand the anxiety Dave was experiencing. He was faced with possibility of losing a good dog, as well as his son's favorite companion and playmate.

Dave said, "I looked into the distant fence-row and saw Barkey." "I called his name and he did not come to me." Knowing something was wrong, I hurried as fast as I could. As I approached him I could hear him whimpering in a very helpless frightened voice. As if to say, please, please, help me. "I expected to find him caught in the fence by his collar, as this sometimes happens."

But, upon arriving at the fence-row, to his dismay Dave found Barkey caught in a fox trap. Instead of being caught in the fence, his front leg was held securely by the trap. The jaws of the trap held him tightly and he was in extreme pain. When Barkey looked up and saw Dave, he whimpered in recognition. He was glad to see him, but also very scared. Not knowing if Dave had set the trap or someone else. He knew that he was hurting very badly and wanted free of the trap and the pain he was experiencing. But, just being found had to be somewhat comforting.

When attempting to open the jaws of the trap, Barkey tried to bite anyone or anything that got near the area of his pain. Gaining his trust was essential. Barkey needed reassurance that no further harm was intended. As Dave gently and softly talked to him, he became calmer. He was watching him and listening to this master's voice. At this time a bond was re-established.

Taking a giant leap of faith, Dave reached to unlatch the jaws of the trap. Thank God it opened and Barkey was set free. He was hurting, but very contented knowing he had been rescued. Instead of hearing the sounds of his joyous barking, you now heard him whimpering with his obvious pain.

Dave picked him up and gently carried him back to the vehicle. Just like our Heavenly Father will carry us in our pain and grief when we are faced with circumstances we cannot carry alone. All we need to do is ask for His help.

As Barkey got caught in the jaws of the fox trap, we can so easily get caught in the jaws of the traps Satan sets for us each day. In I Peter 5:8 God's word tells us to "Be self-controlled and alert. Your enemy the devil prowls around like a roaring lion looking for someone to devour."

By listening to the calming voice of his earthly master, Barkey was set free. When we listen to the gentle voice of our Heavenly Master, Jesus, who softly and tenderly calls us, we too can be set free of the traps that Satan sets.

We should be listening for Jesus' voice during our times of prayer and Bible reading. When we need guidance or protection, we should heed His voice and follow His leading to avoid getting caught in Satan's traps.

Answered

*"In my distress I cried unto the Lord,
and he heard me."
Psalm 120: 1*

Answered Prayer

It was a hot humid day in mid August. So hot that you felt as wilted as the flowers that suffered because of the extreme heat. My husband and I got up early in the morning. We took our showers and prepared to begin our day. We had agreed to take Dad for a mid-morning doctor's appointment in the next town. As we stepped from our air-conditioned home and walked to our car in the garage, my husband exclaimed, "I don't know why we bothered to take showers this morning." "With this heat, I'm drenched in sweat."

We got into our vehicle and turned on the air-conditioner. Soon it was cool and comfortable. We drove to my parent's home, prepared to pick up Dad and Mom to go to the scheduled appointment. Arriving at their home, we noted that Dad had pulled his vehicle (an old Chevy Suburban) from the garage and had turned it facing out the lane. We looked at each other and simultaneously said, "Pap is going to want to drive."

Dad had serious heart problems. Due to his medication and the changes that a heart condition does to the body, he did not mind the heat as we did. He was always feeling cold. Sometimes, he wore his long thermal underwear in the summer months and always long-sleeved shirts. Needless to say he did not use air-conditioning in his home or vehicle.

Dad and Mom were ready to go. They were watching down the road for our arrival. As soon as our vehicle was in sight, Pap got into his vehicle and started the engine. Just as we had said to each other earlier, "Pap wants to drive." My husband and I looked at each other at the same time and said, "In this heat." We knew we were facing a difficult day if we allowed him to drive but even more difficult if we did not. My husband said, "O.K. Pap, you can drive today." We parked our vehicle and got into his. My husband got in the front seat beside Pap. Mom and I got in the back seat.

We left the house with Pap driving to the appointment. We had only gone a short distance when he noticed a Yard Sale sign. His vehicle should have had a bumper sticker that read, "I stop at all Yard Sales." He loved to check out each one and chat with the people there.

He would purchase small items that he thought he could make a dollar profit on at his next yard sale. He was always looking for scrap wood, small pieces of various metals, leftover paint, anything that was considered junk to others. To Pap these articles were treasures. He loved to build birdhouses. Being retired he spent a lot of time making unique creations. You would find him in his workshop transforming the pieces of his treasures (what was considered junk to others) into beautiful birdhouses.

Just as Jesus can take the junk of our lives and transform us into something beautiful if we will allow Him.

I remember Pap and I would take his bird-houses to our local community yard sales. He would have a fair price marked on each one, but if someone remarked about how much they liked a certain one. Pap would say, "You can have it." This was especially true of parents with small children. I often said to him, "Pap how do you expect to make any money today?" He would reply, "I don't' care, let them enjoy it." "It didn't cost me much anyway." To him it didn't matter, he just loved making others happy with his creations.

When we got back into the vehicle, Pap talked about all the bargains he had collected and his plans for them. We stopped at several more en route to the doctor's office. We arrived at our destination, a little late, because of all the stops on our way. His name was called, and he went in for his check-up. Having completed his examination, he joined us in the waiting room.

We got back into the vehicle with Pap driving and my husband in the front seat. Mom and I got into the back seat. No sooner did he start the engine then he said, "Let's go to lunch, I'm hungry." Stopping at our favorite restaurant, we ate our lunch.

Soon we were back on the road and home-ward bound. Or so we thought. We hadn't gone very far when Pap decided to take another route home. Yes, you guessed it; he was in search of more yard sales. We found several and Pap collected more of his "trea-sures" for birdhouse making.

We chatted for awhile and then Mom and I dozed off in the back seat. It had been a long day and we were tired. My husband and Pap continued to chat in the front seat. Suddenly we were awakened by a loud crash. We looked up just as we knocked down a tree. I heard Mom cry out, "Jesus, help us." His word says, "The angel of the Lord encampeth round about them that fear him, and delivereth them" (Psalm 34: 7). When we are afraid, we can turn for comfort to our heavenly Father, whose eyes are always on us and whose ears are open to our cries. God sends His angels to guide us, protect us and comfort us when we call out for His help.

Thank God, Pap insisted on driving his big old heavy Chevy Suburban that morning. It knocked down tree after tree, just like a bulldozer. Unlike our vehicle would have done. We would have been driving a mid-sized much lighter vehicle. The heaviness of Pap's Suburban just pushed the trees down, creating a path until it was stopped by a very large tree.

It seemed like hours, but it was probably only minutes when we came to a sudden stop. We were at the side of a huge drop-off, approximately fifty feet deep. If we would have continued we would have gone down the embankment, and our vehicle would not have been visible from the road.

Depending on our condition, we could have been there for days. Jesus sure did help us, just as He promises He will. All we have to do is ask Him.

We were all O.K. physically, but very shaken up. Pap said, "I must have dozed off." My husband said, "Yes, you did." "I was talking to you and you didn't answer me." "I looked over at you and saw you were not alert." "We were heading off the road towards a deep hole with stagnate water and large rocks at the bottom." It was a sinkhole that had expanded to the depth of fifty feet. It was also approximately forty or fifty feet in diameter. "I tried to get the vehicle back on the road, but was unable to."

We weren't sure what we were going to do. We didn't have a cell phone. We just sat there for awhile asking each other "are you O.K.?" Talking about what we should do, and allowing our nerves to calm.

While we were discussing this, a vehicle stopped and the driver asked if we were O.K. Imagine our surprise when the driver was their grandson. He said, "I don't usually travel this road, but I forgot something and was returning home to get it. This is a shorter route to my home." "I recognized your vehicle in the field and stopped to make sure you were not in need of help."

Thank God for His love and protection again that day. Mom had called to Jesus for help, and He kept His promise by keeping us from injury, and providing a way home for us. As the Bible says, "God is our refuge and strength, a very present help in trouble" (Psalm 46:1).

God promises that we are never beyond His reach. He will meet our needs and care for us. All we need to do in our time of trouble is call His name. Just as God took care of Joshua and Israel and helped them conquer the Promised Land of Canaan, He will take care of us today if we choose to serve Him.

Pap has since passed away. We keep his memory alive with several of the birdhouses he made. When we look at them we think of God's help and protection. They have become our treasures and a constant remembrance of His love and answered prayer.

Unlikely Angel

"For he shall give his angels charge over thee, to keep thee in all thy ways."
Psalm 91:11

Unlikely Angel

Two young ladies and I, who worked together at the same Agency, were instructed to attend a meeting in another state. The youngest of the three volunteered to drive the four hours to our destination. We were looking for the hotel where reservations had been made for us.

It was a beautiful hot sunny day, as we set out to an experience of a lifetime we never expected in our wildest dreams to occur. As we entered the city, our hotel was visible in the distance. But, we had no idea how to get to it from where we were located. The driver pulled into a service station and asked directions. The meeting was to be held at that location. The service station attendant told the driver to continue on this road for approximately four or five miles and make a turn onto Bridge Street. He said that would lead us to the hotel.

As we continued on our way, she drove slowly because of the direct sunlight. Shielding our eyes with our hand, battling the sun, trying desperately to read the names printed on each street sign we approached. Looking for the street name where the attendant had said to make a turn. Having traveled five miles, we still had not seen the street he had told us to look for. The brightness of the sun caused a glare on the next sign located at the top of a hill and the name was not visible. No one in the car remembered if the person at the station had said turn right or left, only that they were to look for Bridge Street.

Upon entering a very busy intersection, a quick decision had to be made. Should we turn, right, left, or continue going straight? Unfortunately, the wrong decision was made. Suddenly we found ourselves in a part of the city where we were told later that no one should go unprotected and never at night. Signs of heavy drug usage and prostitution were everywhere. People young and old were just milling the streets. It was a very run-down neighborhood. It definitely was not a safe environment for three young ladies driving a vehicle with an out-of-state license plate. It was very apparent we were lost, as we continually drove around and around in the city. We were trying desperately to find a street that would lead out of the city and back to the main highway.

After what seemed like hours of driving around, trying to locate a way out. The driver decided to pull over and ask for directions. This was definitely not a neighborhood where you should do that. But, the driver was scared and desperate. Pulling the vehicle to the side of the street, she asked a young man how to get out of this area, and back to the main highway.

While talking with him, the other two occupants in the car observed several groups of young men converging from the front and rear of the vehicle. Needless to say, it was a very frightful time. As they approached us, it was apparent they were not members of the local welcoming committee. By the looks of the situation, they were members of a gang and they knew they were talking to three young ladies lost in a city they knew nothing about.

Suddenly, a souped-up Chevy, and a driver with long hair and hippie-type dress pulled up beside our vehicle. He said to the driver, "Follow me." Turning to the other ladies she asked, "What should I do?" To which they replied, "What choice do we have?" "Just follow him."

Thank God he led us safely out of the city and to our destination. Thinking back on the situation I feel that God had sent one of his angels to protect us. He did not look like what I thought an angel would look like, but sometimes God sends them in the most unlikely forms.

God sends his angels when He knows we cannot take care of ourselves and are in need of His help. Sometimes they are an unseen source of help from which God's children can take courage when facing any crisis that we may encounter. On other occasions they come to assist us in human form. Hebrews

1: 14 calls them "ministering spirits", and they are instantly responsive to God's command.

When we were safely out of that part of the city, the driver of the souped-up Chevy showed us his badge, He said, "I'm an undercover policeman and you ladies were very fortunate I spotted your vehicle driving around in the city." He emphasized to them "not ever to travel through that area unprotected again and never at night." He said, "It is a very unsafe section of the city."

He was the rescuer sent for three frightened young ladies, whom had just escaped a very dangerous encounter. God sends his angels to protect us when we are in need of them; sometimes in the most unlikely forms. We did not know who the rescuer was or how he was lead to us on that day. We just thanked God that someone was there to help when protection was needed. We never know what type of messenger God will send to us in our time of need and the way He keeps His eyes on us, with His protecting arms around us at all times. May we always give God the praise he deserves, especially in times when His presence is felt and known to be the source of our protection.

When we pulled into the parking lot of our hotel, one of the ladies commented about a really nice sports car parked there. With the ordeal just encountered fresh in our minds, another of the ladies remarked, "That person sure is brave or unaware of the dangers of driving that nice car to this area." "I sure hope the entire city is not like the area we just came from."The following morning the nice sports car was setting on concrete blocks and had been completely stripped. The windows were shattered and the wheels were gone. There was nothing but a shell of the classy sports car that had been there the previous day.

Seeing the sports car totally destroyed and experiencing the "lost in the wrong part of the city ordeal" we were anxious to complete our meetings and begin our journey back to the safe haven of our homes. We drove away from that city thanking God for His love, mercy, and protection allowing us to enjoy another day. He is relentless in His love for His children — ever pursuing, ever present, and ever guiding us no matter where we may go, He will go with us. God has said in Hebrews 13:5, "I will never leave thee, nor forsake thee."

His Presence

"Yea, though I walk through the valley
of the shadow of death, I will fear no evil:
for thou art with me;
thy rod and thy staff they comfort me."
Psalm 23: 4

His Presence

It was a cool day in October several years ago, when my husband and I received a phone call from the daughter of a dear friend of ours. She said that her mother had been taken to the hospital, and was not doing very well. She suffered from an incurable illness, and experienced many painful days in her life, which resulted in hospitalization many times during the year.

We were very close to her and her husband. They lived in another state. Most weekends, for approximately four years when they were able, they would come and spend time with us. I never had a sister, only six brothers. She became that sister. She was a loving, caring and wonderful person. We enjoyed many great times of fun and fellowship together. We told them that they had an open invitation to our home.

We would spend hours talking, playing card games, and enjoying each other's company. As our friendship grew we began to attend church together. It was in our small little church that they both came to know and love the Lord. This increased the closeness of our relationship to each other. We would spend hours discussing the Bible and the sermon we had just listened to that Sunday morning.

It was such a joy for each of us to grow in the knowledge and love of Jesus. They became such a blessing to my husband and me.

Several years passed and they were not able to come to visit as often. Her husband's health began to fail so they stayed home. The drive to our home became too difficult for him. We went to visit them, but it was not the same as having them stay in our home and share in Sunday worship services with us.

We discussed building an addition onto our home and having them move into the rooms that would be adjoining. But, they were reluctant to leave the security of their own doctors, home, and children.

One day we received a call that he passed away. We were very saddened and shared in her grief at the loss of her husband and our brother in the Lord. But we found comfort and peace in knowing that now he was in His presence. It is better not to know what the future holds, but to know the One who holds the future. If we knew, we would want to give up when we are faced with such difficult circumstances. Sometimes it's God's way of getting our attention. It forces us to rely on His presence to comfort and guide us through those times. Trusting this will result in a closer walk and a dependence on Him that we may not have developed if life was all mountain top experiences, without any valleys to go through.

After his death, his wife felt so alone. She would come to visit us when she was able and spend several months with us. We really enjoyed the time we spent with her. One day, when she was staying with us she got very sick so we called her son and daughter. They came and took her back to her home so she would be near her doctors and the hospital.

The morning we received the call that she had been hospitalized, we did not hesitate to drive to the hospital. We left with thoughts of returning that same day. When we got there, she was as ill as we had ever seen her. She weighed less than eighty pounds, and looked so alone in that hospital bed. She could no longer speak but she wrote "I'm dying" on a notepad and handed it to my husband. We read it and looked at her. She mouthed to us, "please don't leave me alone." There was no way we could leave her bedside. We stayed there reading scripture, singing songs, and reminiscing about days of childhood and pleasant memories of times we had spent together. She did not respond, but we felt she heard us. Occasionally, she would open her eyes and look at one of us.

This continued for approximately three weeks. We did not go home, but stayed at the hospital in one of the waiting rooms. My husband and I would take turns sleeping on the recliners that were provided. One of us was always by her side.

The presence of the Lord was very real to us, and we had strength that could only have come from Him. Several of the hospital staff suggested that we should go home, rest, and return the next day. But with God's help we were determined not to leave her bedside as she had requested of us. For weeks she laid very unresponsive in the hospital bed. The hospital staff wondered what was keeping her alive. Because of her illness, they had administered heavy doses of pain medication.

One afternoon my brother and his wife came to visit her. He prayed with her and then said, "Save me a seat in heaven." She looked right at him and responded with "I will", and said his name. That sure was all the encouragement we needed to give us the strength to stay as long as necessary.

After that happened she closed her eyes and lay there for several more days unresponsive. We continued to talk, pray, and sing to her. My husband was reminiscing with her about the days when they attended Sunday school together. He said, "Do you remember the song, "I'll Be a Sunbeam?" He started to sing it and said, "What's the rest of the words?" "I forget." Suddenly, she sat up in bed and sang as clear as a bell the words to the song "I'll be a Sunbeam."

> Jesus wants me for a sunbeam,
> To shine for Him each day;
> In every way to please Him,
> At home, at school, at play.
> A sunbeam, a sunbeam,
> Jesus wants me for a sunbeam;
> A sunbeam, a sunbeam,
> I'll be a sunbeam for Him.

She definitely was a testimony to everyone present in her room that morning. The hospital staff was in total amazement, because they felt that she should have passed away three days ago. There was no way to deny the power of the Lord.

Several days later the staff asked that we leave the room, because they were attending to her needs. My husband and I went to the cafeteria to eat breakfast. When we were returning to her room, her son met us. He said that his mother had just passed away. We were very sad at our loss but have so many wonderful memories of her to cherish.

We will always remember how the Holy Spirit guided us at a very difficult time in our lives. He was invisible to our eyes, but He walked through it with us. Just as Jesus walked with His disciples on earth long ago, so the Holy Spirit walks with us today.

We experienced the presence and power of the Lord that will never be forgotten. When we put our trust in Him we can have peace about whatever situation we are going through.

He said He would never leave us (Hebrews 13: 5). In Matthew 1:23 the Bible states: "Behold, a virgin shall be with child, and shall bring forth a son, and they shall call his name Emmanuel, which being interpreted is, God with us." Even when we don't understand life's painful problems, we can trust God to be near and to work out His purpose for us.

His Healing

"Heal me, O Lord, and I shall be healed;
save me, and I shall be saved:
for thou art my praise."
Jeremiah 17:14

His Healing

As told by Chris Guyer

A very dear friend shared this story with me.

I was working as a Certified Nurse's Assistant at a local nursing home getting to know and love the residents. Each day, I felt I was using the gift God gave me of caring for others and enjoying serving Him in this way.

I am married to a loving husband and we had just joined a local church where we were learning more about the Lord and His Word while enjoying getting to know our church family. Life was really going great for us and we were very happy.

Then one day in September, five years ago, when I came home from work I was very tired. I had an extremely busy day so I went to bed early; praying that I would feel well rested the next morning. But, the next day I noticed that my breast was swollen, red, and warm to the touch. It was also very painful. Fear went through me. Could this be cancer? Working as a nurse's assistant I knew all the signs.

I shared my feelings and my fears with my husband. He told me to make an appointment with my gynecologist right away. He was very concerned. He had commented about how tired I had been looking lately. I called and got an appointment that day. She examined me and said I had an infection in my breast. She prescribed an antibiotic to take for two weeks. I returned for my follow-up appointment at the end of the two weeks. The antibiotics did not show the results she had hoped for. Therefore, a mammogram was performed. It revealed a cloudy area on my breast. This was of great concern for the doctor, so a sonogram was done on that area. The results were also not encouraging.

She called and set up an appointment with a surgeon. He told me I needed to have an M.R.I. done immediately. He said he would know the results in a few days. I knew the prognosis was in God's hand and I prayed for His intervention and guidance. The doctor received the results of the M.R.I. sooner than he had expected.

The next day I received a call that I was to come to his office to review the results of the M.R.I. He discussed them with my husband and me. He said I needed to have a biopsy performed immediately. This report really scared me. But, I was trusting God to help see me through this ordeal I was facing. He answered my prayer, because the surgeon was also a Christian. We all prayed for God to be with me as he performed the procedure.

After reviewing the results, I was informed that I had Ductal Carcinoma breast cancer. This is a very rare type of fast growing cancer. I was so thankful that all of my previous tests had come back so quickly and the diagnosis was made early. I did not have time to wait, because this cancer can spread very rapidly. I knew God's hand was in this circumstance, because test results are not usually known so quickly. It was essential that the doctor knew what he was dealing with and how to treat it.

When the doctor told my husband and me that I had breast cancer, we were both so devastated. Tears welled up in our eyes and we both cried and cried. The doctor put his arms around us both and said he would be praying for me. He said, "I am a Christian and I know that you must keep the faith and a positive attitude." It will help you to go through this ordeal.

Dr. Norman Vincent Peale, minister to millions, stated in his message regarding positive thinking "that he viewed it as a values-centered way of life empowered by faith in God, faith in oneself, and faith in the future."

After we left the doctor's office, reality really began to set in. I was a jumble of emotions: angry, scared, bitter, and somewhat hopeful. I had seen so many of the results of cancer.

I told my husband that I wanted a divorce; because I did not want the man I love to have to go through this with me. He said, "No, we took our marriage vows to love and cherish in sickness and health, and I will not abandon you at the first encounter we have with sickness." I thanked God for his love and understanding.

The surgeon called an oncologist and scheduled an appointment for me. God was still working in my favor, because he was able to arrange a time in less than one week. Sometimes, it takes months to see a specialist.

He told me I would be starting Chemotherapy in a few days. I was very scared and depressed about it. I had known others who that gone through therapy and had gotten deathly sick. I was so worried that I would not be able to make it through the upcoming sessions.

My husband reminded me about the words in James 5: 14, 15. The Bible says, "Is any sick among you? let him call for the elders of the church; and let them pray over him, anointing him with oil in the name of the Lord: and the prayer of faith shall save the sick, and the Lord shall raise him up; and if he had committed sins, they shall be forgiven him."

We contacted our pastor the day before I was scheduled to start the Chemotherapy treatments and asked to be anointed. I went to church that Sunday, but I was not in a worshipful mood. I was very depressed. After the anointing service my spirits were lifted and I had a peace about the treatments I would be starting the following day. I remembered the words of the surgeon on the day I received my diagnosis. He had told me to keep the faith and a positive attitude. I now felt that with God's help, I could endure the days of treatments I had to go through.

It was in the autumn of the year, and the leaves were beautiful shades of red, yellow, and orange. God had been busy with His paintbrush. I asked my husband if he wanted to go for a drive through the mountains and see the beauty of God's great creation. He agreed that would be a nice thing to do. We had a wonderful time and a day we will always remember and cherish. I felt a peace and calmness I had not experienced before.

Early the next morning, we drove to the hospital for my first Chemotherapy treatment. I was required to have four sessions of treatment. Each session was for two weeks. This consisted of two hours of Chemotherapy every Monday, and then Tuesday through Friday I received a shot in the stomach in order to keep my white blood cell count up and to boost my weakened immune system. Every day for eight weeks as we drove the twenty-five mile round trip I got sicker and sicker after each session.

By the end of the second week of treatment my hair began to fall out. I could take my hands through my hair and it came out in clumps. This upset me very much. I would cry continually and get more depressed as I had to face each treatment. I did not want to look at myself in the mirror, nor did I want anyone else to see me. Especially, I was embarrassed for my husband to see me bald.

Two days after my first eight weeks of treatments I received a complete body scan.

Two days later I received the news that the cancer had not spread throughout my body. I felt I had received another miracle from God and an answer to many prayers.

I was scheduled for surgery. I was scared and not looking forward to having to go through it. The prognosis was that I needed a complete mastectomy. Again, I was anointed with oil and the elders of our church prayed with my husband and me. All my family and friends were present praying for me and giving me support.

My pastor and my husband both commented that they saw no fear in my eyes. I had a calmness and peace about the surgery, because I knew my faith was strong and God would see me through.

After the surgery, the surgeon called my family into the hallway to discuss the results. My husband asked how the surgery went. He told him it went very well. He was truly amazed, because he did not find the mass that he had anticipated he would find. I had just received another miracle from God.

I was so happy and relieved. My hair had just started to grow back and I was starting to feel much better about myself.

Then the doctor said, "You will have to go through more Chemotherapy treatments." Again, each session would be for two weeks. But this time the treatment would be increased to four hours of Chemotherapy every Monday, then Tuesday through Friday I received a shot in the stomach to keep my white blood cell count up.

Deep depression set in and I did not want to be with any of my friends. I just wanted to be alone with my feelings of misery and despair. Again, I lost all my hair and was really tired of feeling so sick and weak all the time. I just wanted this nightmare to end.

My husband really had to urge me to finish the Chemotherapy. Finally, I finished the treatments and I was so glad when they were over.

The doctor told me I would have a two week break and then would begin radiation treatments. I was required to have a total of thirty-two sessions. This was every day for thirty-two days.

My hair started to grow back and I started to feel a little better each day. I wasn't sick, but I had a lot of side effects to overcome. I felt weak and had a lot of muscle aches in my body, especially in my legs.

Five years later, I still have side effects. It was very hard working through losing a body part. I felt like I was not a whole woman. I still get periods of weakness and pain in the area of my body that is missing. But, thanks to God He is helping me and I'm growing stronger in my faith.

Every year on the date of my surgery, my husband and I go again for a drive through the mountains to see the beauty of the fall foliage and view God's great creation. We are reminded of His greatness and the miracles that were performed on that day years ago. Each time we go the colors seem brighter and more beautiful. It gives us peace and hope to face each new day.

I told our children and grandchildren about what their grandma had gone through. My oldest granddaughter, who was eight years old at the time, was required to write an essay for a school project. It was to be about the person that had the greatest influence in her life. Following is a copy of that essay.

"The person who has had the greatest influence on my life is my Grandma Chris, because she has had breast cancer and was still happy during it. She went through so much medication her doctors prescribed, she was bald, the doctors had to do surgery, and she was still happy during it. She got a little bit more tired and couldn't do as much as she used to for awhile and got a little upset, but she still stayed happy during cancer.

Now a few years later, she goes every six months to get checkups on her cancer and she's as happy as ever. She's doing some of her old hobbies, she's spending time with my brother, sister, and me, and she just got two more bundles of joy to spend time with from her daughter, or my aunt. She wants us to spend lots of time as we can with our cousins and likes to take us places.

My Grandma Chris is the strongest, happiest, person I ever knew in my life. She went through so much and never worried. She was upset when she first found out, but she got better I think for us. My grandma is the greatest influence in my life."

My husband and I did not know Chris and her husband when they were going through these trying times. We attended the same church, but we were just acquaintances. Since then we have become very good friends. We ride bikes together on our local bike trail. Sharing with people we meet on the trail about how great and wonderful a God we serve.

Chris and I also play in our church bell choir. We have spent many enjoyable hours playing music for God's glory and pleasure.

We both are members of our church's Prayer Shawl Ministry. The purpose of this ministry is to knit or crochet shawls to give to persons in need spiritually or physically. I've watched her crocheting these shawls as she experienced pain in her arms and fingers. But, she continued with no thought of her own pain. She concentrated on the fact that giving the shawl to someone in need would bring a smile to his or her face. She never lets her experience with cancer get her down. She enjoys the gift of life the Lord has given to her each new day.

Her experience with cancer could have left her bitter, but it did not. It made her faith stronger and her walk closer to the Lord. She knew she was not equipped to handle the problems she was faced with, but God was. She believed as He said in Psalm 55:22, "Cast thy burden upon the Lord, and he shall sustain thee: he shall never suffer the righteous to be moved."

She has an upbeat personality and is always ready to lend a helping hand to whomever, wherever and whatever the need may be.

She knows that her healing came from God and she is so very thankful for that blessing. She is an inspiration and encouragement to others by her actions. It is a real joy to know her and her husband as our brother and sister in the Lord and to grow in love and friendship together.

God's Willing Servant

*"Therefore all things whatsoever ye
would that men should do to you,
do ye even so to them:
for this is the law and the prophets."*
Matthew 7:12

God's Willing Servant

On a very hot, humid July afternoon, I presented the story entitled, "With God's Help", and gave my testimony at a local assisted living facility. A testimony of how God will use ordinary everyday people to do His work on earth. All He requires is that we be a willing vessel to be used for His purpose.

When my husband and I arrived, the residents were eating their lunch. As I prepared to give the presentation, I was observing one of the young ladies employed there. We'll call her "Angel." While watching her, thoughts came to my mind that this young lady was truly an everyday angel. She was helping to serve and meet the needs of each one. I noted the smile with which she helped each person. Each had different needs and wants, all with different personalities, but as she helped them she displayed the "same" willing attitude.

They were finished with lunch and it was time for the program to begin. Several of the residents came into the activity room where they were instructed to meet. But, some went to their rooms just out of habit. Angel noticed that this had happened. Not wanting anyone to miss the presentation, she went to each room of at least five to eight of the residents. She personally assisted each one so they would not miss the story and testimony. Still she had that smile and jovial attitude as each was escorted into the room and seated.

When the program began, Angel found a seat among the residents. But, as she listened to the story and testimony I noted her watchful eyes roaming throughout the room to see if anyone needed anything. The Bible says in Isaiah 40:11, "He shall feed his flock like a shepherd: he shall gather the lambs with his arm…" Just as Jesus watches over His flock Angel displayed the same attributes as she lovingly cared for her flock.

What amazed me most was that she had just been informed that she was required to perform double-duty that evening. She would only be home a few hours and then would return to work. Knowing this, instead of being concerned about her own well being she was thinking of the residents. She stayed hours after her regular tour of duty was completed — just to make sure every resident had the opportunity to enjoy the story and testimony.

At the close of the program, I heard her lovingly tell everyone that she would see him or her in a couple of hours. Because of the extreme heat that day, she cautioned them not to go outside for long periods of time. Also, reminding them the importance of drinking plenty of fluids to prevent de-hydration.

We may serve for years in a place where no one notices or even cares about anything we say or do while living on earth. But God sees and cares. One day, when we reach our eternal home,…"then shall every man have praise of God." (I Corinthians 4: 5). In the meantime, verse 2 of that same chapter requires that we remain faithful. God will reward us for our faithfulness.

Jesus wants us to submit to each other in humble, loving service. He wants us to take the time to lend a helping hand where needed. Even though His time was overwhelmed with His ministry, He found time to serve others. Should we do any less? The only appropriate motivation for service to others is to love them — just as Jesus modeled love when He washed the feet of His disciples. The Bible tells us in Ephesians 6:7, "With good will doing service, as to the Lord, and not to men."

Angel thought only of the needs of others. She modeled Jesus as Philippians 2:4 instructs, "Look not every man on his own things, but every man also on the things of others."

I can only imagine how much happier this world would be if it were not such a me first world and more people would just be everyday angels or God's willing servants to the people they come in contact with each day.

Divine Intervention

For He is always there,
behind you, beside you
and before you!

Divine Intervention

Julie was a young woman whose greatest desire was to be a mother. She had grown up as the oldest in her family. At a very early age she learned the chores and the joys of caring for her younger siblings. While most of her friends were playing pretend feeding and changing of baby dolls, Julie was feeding and changing real babies and loving every minute of it. It seemed like at a very early age God had given her this ability to love and nurture young children.

She spent many hours bouncing them on her knee, rocking them to sleep and singing lullabies to them. When they grew older she enjoyed playing various board games, reading stories and baking cookies. She recalled that one of their favorite action games was "Simon Says." She loved being a little mother and caring for and entertaining them.

Soon Julie met and married a very nice young man. He was the man of her childhood dreams. They both wanted children very much. But the years began to pass and there were no children. Seven years had passed and finally Julie noted that she had begun to put on some extra weight. In addition, she awoke feeling sick and nauseous at the start of her day. Could it possibly be "morning sickness?" Oh how she prayed that it was. All she could do was imagine the joy of holding her very own little bundle of joy.

She told her husband of her suspicions and he suggested that they make an appointment with a doctor immediately. The earliest appointment available was in three weeks. She could hardly wait for the day to arrive. It seemed like forever but finally they were on their way to the doctor's office. The doctor confirmed that Julie indeed was going to have a baby.

She and her husband were ecstatic with the thought of a precious gift of a child from God. The months passed and it was evident that Julie was going to be a mother. She was so happy to be gaining weight now that she knew the reason why.

The second month of the pregnancy problems began and she had to spend several months in the hospital, then would be released and re-admitted. This continued for the next five months. As time passed she began to feel sicker and weaker. A very dear friend told her that even though the doctor had said she was pregnant her stomach did not look normal. At her next appointment she decided to tell her doctor what the friend had said.

He said he had noticed this and was keeping a close watch on it until tests could be performed. Because of the problems with the pregnancy it was not possible to do any tests in the early stages. The next month the doctor ordered tests to be done. The results showed that in addition to being pregnant Julie also had a very rare form of tumor growing in her stomach. The doctor gave her some medication and said he would watch very closely the growth of the fetus.

Several days later she awoke with severe pain and was rushed to the hospital. She lay in the hospital very sick for several weeks. Late one afternoon the doctor came in and talked to her husband. He said, "You have to make a choice." "If we don't abort this baby your wife may not make it." She is not strong enough to continue to carry this baby. The life of both mother and child are in serious danger. I want to try a different medication tonight. If it does not help then I need to know your answer early tomorrow morning.

Her husband was faced with the realization that he could lose his wife or the child they both wanted so much. Possibility both, but his wife had a better chance of survival if the fetus was aborted. The doctor would not make that decision. He would only state his professional opinion and recommendation. He said, "I need your answer in the morning."

Faced with such a decision her husband prayed for guidance. He believed that God gives life and He takes it away. Only God had the right to make such a decision. He loved his wife very much and also their unborn child. That night there was very little sleep for him as he struggled with what the doctor had said to him. Morning finally came and he went to the hospital, not sure of what he would be facing.

The doctor was in Julie's room when he arrived. He told him that he had been called in because she awoke this morning with premature labor pains and aborted both the tumor and the fetus. He said it was for the best because after seeing the condition of the fetus, the child would have been severely deformed. This was because the nourishment that should have been feeding the fetus had been going to the tumor and both were growing. That was what caused the abnormality of the fetus and would have been the reason for the deformity.

They were very thankful that such an extraordinary event was manifested by God intervening in their lives that they were not forced to have to make such a decision.

Julie spent several weeks in the hospital and was given numerous pints of blood. Each day she gained some of her strength back. Weeks later the doctor came into the room while her husband was there and said I need to talk to both of you.

He began by reminding both of them about how sick Julie had been and how weak her system was at this time. He said," I know how much you both want children, but my recommendation is that you do not become pregnant for at least a year." He said, "Julie your body is just too weak to carry a child full-term." They were very disappointed but knew that the doctor's advice was for the best.

Approximately fourteen months later Julie started to have morning sickness again. In her third month she miscarried. She and her husband were totally devastated. They both wanted a child so much. It was hard for them to accept, but they knew that it was God's timing and not their own. For reasons unknown to them He did not choose to give them the desires of their heart at this time. They were traumatized and disappointed but very grateful that they still had each other.

They believed that God heard and would answer their prayers in His time. God already knows the plans he has for each one of us. You simply have to wait for His timing to bring it to you!

The waiting is the difficult part, but this is how God develops patience and faith in you. You simply have to have faith, trust and belief that God has your life completely in His hands and that He will answer you in His time and in His way.

And not only does God have a set plan and a set future for your life — but He also has a set timetable in which all of these plans will manifest in your life. You must learn to have complete faith in the Lord. The Bible says, "Delight thyself also in the Lord; and he shall give thee the desires of thine heart. Commit thy way unto the Lord; trust also in him; and he shall bring it to pass. ... Rest in the Lord, and wait patiently for Him" (Psalm 37:4, 5, 7).

It was very hard for them to do, but they knew they had to let go and let God. God would come in with the breakthrough on His time schedule — not theirs!

Several years past and their love for each other grew. As they were cultivating their relationship, God rewarded them with another pregnancy.

When Julie and her husband went to the doctor he recommended that she receive a monthly hormone shot. This would improve her ability to carry the baby full-term. Each visit the doctor said the pregnancy was progressing normally.

Nine months later they were rewarded for their patience and faith in the Lord. Julie and her husband received the bundle of joy they had prayed for.

They were rewarded with a healthy baby boy. He weighed less than five pounds but was perfect in every way!

Mother's Bible

*"Study to shew thyself approved unto God,
a workman that needeth not to be ashamed,
rightly dividing the word of truth."*
II Timothy 2: 15

Mother's Bible

Mother's Bible is filled with pearls of wisdom. She has collected these throughout her life and written them on the pages of her Bible. The one I am sharing is about judging. She searched the scriptures to find the answer to a problem facing a small town. Following are a few scriptures that related to that topic.

A small town had scheduled male strippers for entertainment and Christians were voicing their opposition in the local newspapers. Other persons responded to the articles writing that the so-called Christians were not acting like Christians. They said that they were judging and casting stones and they did not have the right to do this. Many people will seemingly use this to justify their sinful actions.

I Peter 1: 15, 16 God's word instructs us to be holy. The scripture says, "But as he which hath called you is holy, so be ye holy in all manner conversation; Because it is written, Be ye holy; for I am holy." Because of God's grace, we can be agents of His holiness, for He now dwells within us. We should seek as Jesus did, for ways to be a source of holiness to those around us.

We have to look very carefully when others say that Christians are judging. In Matthew 7: 15, 17 Jesus said to beware of false prophets. He talks about good trees bringing forth good fruit and corrupt trees bringing forth evil fruit. In His word He already has given us the right to judge the actions of evil.

In Ephesians 5: 11 the Bible says, "And have no fellowship with the unfruitful works of darkness, but rather reprove them." Again, the Bible says: "Beware lest any man spoil you through philosophy and vain deceit, after the tradition of men, after the rudiments of the world, and not after Christ" (Colossians 2: 8).

When Jesus has already judged something was wrong and a sin, we are not wrong in judging the sinful actions of a person if it is contrary to the word of God.

"For the Lord giveth wisdom; out of his mouth cometh knowledge and understanding" (Proverbs 2: 6). Keeping our love for Christ and His wisdom preeminent is a primary objective for us if we want to live to satisfy God throughout the course of our life here on this earth.

Mother searched for knowledge by reading the scriptures, as someone looking for hidden treasures. She realized it was more valuable than silver, gold, or rubies. By doing this she gained wisdom from God to live each day of her life. Wisdom is called "a tree of life." This is a symbolic way of describing the blessings of being in a right relationship with God and one that is seeking it. The Bible is a great treasure of wisdom and truth about God, about life, and about eternity.

A wise person can walk through this life with confidence, being assured of the Lord's approval. You can gain knowledge, but wisdom comes from God. The Lord will bless us if we obey Him; and give wisdom, truth, and His love to all that choose to walk in His way as His children.

Mother's Bible is filled with pearls of wisdom that God has given to her. Every time her Bible is opened, you will find new hidden treasures from God's Word written on the pages. They all relate to her daily walk and personal relationship with Jesus Christ.

She searched diligently to find these rare treasures to gain insight and wisdom from God's word. Wisdom is discovered and enjoyed only if you are diligent, devoted, and determined to seek it. Strive to grow in God's wisdom every day and this will nurture a love and trust relationship with Him.

In order to gain spiritual fitness you must walk daily with the Lord. This is an exercise program that has eternal rewards.

Breinigsville, PA USA
21 February 2011
255941BV00001B/2/P